4D
WARFARE

CASTALIA HOUSE

4D
WARFARE

A DOCTRINE FOR A NEW
GENERATION OF POLITICS

JACK POSOBIEC

CASTALIA HOUSE

4D Warfare: A Doctrine for a New Generation of Politics

Jack Posobiec

Published by Castalia House
Kouvola, Finland
www.castaliahouse.com

Contents

Introduction

This is your introduction to *4D Warfare*.

Welcome to warfare in the information age, where politics and societal and cultural struggles are played out in a new arena that is called the Information Environment.

"4D Warfare" stands for *four-dimensional* warfare. 4D Warfare is sometimes wrongly referred to as "trolling" by the misinformative mainstream media, because most mainstream political reporters lack the education and the real-world experience to understand what they are writing about. Instead of writing about the strategies employed by the various political factions, they simply promote the side that confirms their preconceived bias—which is largely leftist—then dismiss everyone else as "crazy" due to their deficient understanding of any perspective that challenges their worldview.

The term "4D Warfare" is derived from the term "4GW," which stands for Fourth-Generation Warfare. Fourth-generation warfare is based on the premise that there are multiple layers of warfare in the battlespace as it exists today in the 21st century. While the concept is a relatively new one, multi-layered conflicts have been going on for centuries. Even so, it is only in recent years that military leaders and strategists have begun taking into account the diverse forms of combat that take place *beyond the physical battlefield* in a conceptual battlefield that primarily exists in the realm of ideas and perceptions.

What *4D Warfare* provides is an understanding, analysis, and instructional manual for 4D warriors to go forth and wage political warfare across all fronts of the Information Environment, including both digital and physical spaces. In 21st century conflicts, what happens on the ground is not always the most influential factor. A greater impact is often found in the way events are later portrayed by media and social media and eventually accepted as fact by the public. Sometimes, as you will see, the actual facts on the ground are not accurately described by the narrative that the mainstream media pushes as the official story.

In 4DW, the narrative is all. At its core, 4DW is the battle to control the narrative.

In this book, we take the best practices and lessons of 4GW from the world of military strategy, national security, and modern defense tactics, and apply them to the political and cultural issues of our day. These techniques and tactics and practices also apply to almost anything in life, which is important, for as we have seen, the political Left has sought to politicize everything from bathrooms to fast food to immigration to sports.

One form of 4D Warfare is memetic warfare. Many have studied this grand and ancient art. I hope that by the end of this book, you will be able to perfect your memeing to unprecedented levels of winning.

What we all want is for the United States of America to return to the ideals and principles of the Founding, and at the same time, to preserve our hard-won freedoms and civil liberties. We wish the same for all nations who have found freedom.

Many in the conservative movement use the threadbare tactic of writing five-thousand-word essays complaining about having been bested once again by the Left. Yes, I do get the irony of complaining about this in an introduction to a book that is more than four times that length, but what *4D Warfare* offers is an effective alternative to these long-failed tactics and strategies. It is a new way of waging the culture wars—and winning!

President Donald Trump is a master of 4D warfare and I would be remiss were I to exclude him from this discussion. Through pugnacious public statements and Twitter posts alone, he generates news cycles, reshapes narratives, and masterfully transforms the attacks on him into tactical and strategic victories.

There is no better example of successful 4D warfare than the election of Donald J. Trump as President of the United States in 2016. One individual stood up to the combined forces of two political parties, the mainstream media, and the global establishment, and won against the odds. He *never* could have accomplished this without his deep inherent understanding of 4D warfare.

In this book I will discuss 4DW tactics that have been employed by the Left and by the Right in the culture war. We'll analyze those that have been successful and review those that have failed. I will show you what to do if you find yourself facing these tactics and I will show you how to make use of them yourself.

By the end of this book, you will be a full-fledged 4D Warrior.

Let's roll!

Chapter 1

The Information Environment

A mind needs books as a sword needs a whetstone.

—Tyrion Lannister

You can see things in the Information Environment, but you cannot see it itself. You can be part of the Information Environment—you can experience the Information Environment—you can even follow it passively as millions do every day... or you can *affect* it.

The "Information Environment" simply means, "all of the readily available information at a given time."

The U.S. Army defines the Information Environment as the aggregate of individuals, organizations, and systems that collect, process, disseminate, or act on information.

Army Field Manual 3-13 is titled, "*Information Operations.*" It states: "Information is an element of combat power. Commanders conduct information operations to apply it. Focused information operations—synchronized with effective information management and intelligence, surveillance, and reconnaissance—enable commanders to gain and maintain information superiority."

Information superiority is achieved when one side has total access to all of the available information and the opposition's access to that information is restricted. This is accomplished through a variety of means—legal and illegal. Hacking or remotely controlling opposition communications devices is a well-known form of affecting the flow of information, but it is not within the scope of this book, nor is any illegal act. Social media is a remarkable barometer for perceiving the Information Environment. Though the lens is skewed, it is almost possible to see the Information Environment itself through Twitter, Facebook, YouTube, Snapchat, Instagram, and other social media applications. Livestreaming apps like Periscope, Facebook Live, and YouTube Live also further this vision.

Numerous factors make up the Information Environment and influence it at any given time—including political, military, economic, social, infrastructure, the physical environment, and timeliness.

Any outlet producing information content is part of the Information Environment, including your favorite TV or Netflix shows, documentaries, the Hollywood box office, music, newspapers, bloggers and, more recently, social media platforms and their corporate owners.

In the American Revolutionary War, control of the Information Environment was one of the factors that brought independence to the British colonies in North America. The British Crown understood the power of control over information, and thereby instituted the Stamp Act. A provision of the tax required printed materials, such as newspapers, to be printed on stamped paper produced in London. As printers were unduly affected by this new law, many colonial newspapers were particularly critical of the act, leading to the heightened political tensions that later gave way to the Revolution itself.

Pamphlets also played a major role in the American Revolution. The most famous of these was *Common Sense*, written in January, 1776, by Thomas Paine. The book is written in an accessible and highly persuasive tone and its sales took off almost immediately. It became a popular bestseller, selling hundreds of thousands of copies in its first few months of publication. It was a tremendous sensation. People were reading aloud from *Common Sense* in taverns and meeting places. In modern terms, *Common Sense* was the first viral sensation in American history. *Common Sense*'s impact was later seen by its important place in the political environment, where it framed and directed the debate of the American colonists who would declare independence just a few months later. It must be understood that *Common Sense* went viral because it fit so well into the Information Environment's primary conversation at hand—the conflict with Great Britain—and because it was a simple summary of the situation. Paine's book presented arguments for independence to a mass audience that was highly receptive due to the circumstances.

Thomas Paine's writing was a massive success because it influenced the Information Environment so much it that it generated a political response. *Common Sense* was not a financial success, unfortunately, because he was cheated by his publishers. I do not expect to be cheated by the publishers of this book, but I have learned from Thomas and I am keeping an eye on you!

Chapter 2

Make it Go Viral

When the snows fall and the white winds blow, the lone wolf dies, but the pack survives.

—Eddard Stark

About three hundred times a day, I am sent a message or article or hashtag or meme from someone asking, "Hey, Jack, can you tweet this? I want it to go viral."

Now, I'm happy to share content for just about anyone. As long as I agree with the message and it's not calling for hatred or bigotry, I will usually share it. But what I don't have any control over is what goes viral and what doesn't. That's not up to me. That's up to the thousands of people who use Twitter as well as the influential Twitter algorithms that determine whether content that is retweeted will appear in someone's timeline or not.

Social media is like riding a wave. News cycles come and go, but it is the waves of reaction to a story in the Information Environment that dictate whether something will go viral or be quickly forgotten. Timing is everything! Never plan hashtags. Never schedule tweets. The best equation to maximize your chances of going viral is equal parts reflexive reactivity and spontaneity. I could post the funniest meme I've ever seen in my life, but it won't go viral unless it somehow relates to the conversation at hand. A viral campaign might contain all the right ingredients, but if it doesn't fit the current conversation, it will fall flat and disappear into the electronic aether.

During the 2016 election, one strategy that was often employed in order to gain visibility was to create a hashtag, then campaign in order to get enough people interested in that hashtag to cause it to trend. As of this writing, it's been months since I bothered trying to create any kind of hashtag campaign because Twitter rarely allows right-wing hashtags to trend anymore. The environment is no longer favorable because the algorithms are hostile.

The ability to make something go viral is determined by social psychology, market analysis, brand awareness, and writing ability. If you don't understand any one of those ingredients or can't apply them correctly, you're unlikely to go viral. You might have the most brilliant idea in the world, but if you need a sixty-seven-tweet-long tweetstorm to make your point, it's not going anywhere. In the military, we had a saying about giving presentations to high-ranking officers: "Be good, be brief, be gone." That's my strategy when it comes to social media.

Recently, Twitter unexpectedly changed its famous 140-character limit to 280 characters. This flies in the face of the Twitter experience, and in my opinion, will ultimately lead to the downfall of the company. The reason is simple. Laconic turns of phrase and pithy, sarcastic comments are why people from all backgrounds love to use Twitter. Yet instead of discussing potential changes with users to find out what they wanted out of their experience, Twitter CEO Jack Dorsey simply waved his hand and forced 280 characters on everyone. It was rather like Apple infuriating its users by doing away with iPhone headphone jacks and the home button.

Tone deafness will not be tolerated in business, and tone deafness will not be tolerated in social media. People just want to share the content they like. Simply put, if you want to make something go viral, you have to make content your audience will enjoy sharing. There isn't any magic to it... there isn't any formula... it's simply grinding away, day after day, making content and breaking stories.

But even with my experience and intellectual understanding of the phenomenon of virality, I still can't tell you which content will go viral and which won't. The truth is that even the experts in a field can't predict the future with any degree of reliability. George Lucas famously bet Stephen Spielberg that his 1977 movie *Star Wars* would be a total flop. He was wrong.

It went viral.

Chapter 3

What are Psy Ops?

Fear cuts deeper than swords.

—Syrio Forel

Two terms you may have heard since the 2016 Presidential election are: "Psyops" and "gaslighting." These psychological manipulation tactics were frequently used by the mainstream media and the D.C. establishment in their failed attempt to prevent Donald Trump from winning the election. Understanding these tactics allows you to better see through them when they are employed. Even when you know what to look for they can be difficult to detect given their intrinsically subversive nature, as well as the way they blend fact with fiction.

Psychological operations (PSYOPs) are planned operations which convey selected information and indicators to audiences in order to influence their emotions, motives, and objective reasoning—and, ultimately, to alter the behavior of governments, organizations, groups, and individuals.

Gaslighting is a form of psychological abuse in which a victim is manipulated into doubting his own memory, perception, and sanity. Instances may range from an abuser's denial that previous abusive incidents ever occurred, to the staging of bizarre events by the abuser with the intention of confusing and disorienting the victim.

Television is an advertising medium, by definition. Television has been weaponized—and never more so than in the 2016 election. Media analyst Dr. Marshall McLuhan famously said, in 1964, "The medium is the message." Dr. McLuhan prophetically explained that the media possesses its own society and social attitudes. For example, a story on a news channel about any particular crime seldom has anything to do with the actual crime being reported. Instead, the news story primarily concerns manipulating a change in public attitude towards the crime and the alleged criminals involved. On television, it is the construction of the narrative that matters rather than the actual facts of any specific story.

Army Field Manual 33-1-1 provides some of the additional objectives of psyops, noting that they are practiced to stimulate dissension within opponents' ranks, undermine confidence in opponents' leadership and aims, lower the morale and efficiency of opponents, encourage disagreement between elements of the opposition that have grievances between each other, and interfere with the opponents' communication systems.

The manual outlines a divide-and-conquer strategy of demoralization and fracturing. When facing a solidly unified force, psyops are used to break up that force and create divisions among its strongest elements.

The mainstream media, including Fox News, appeared to be operating directly out of the *Army Field Manual* on psyops throughout 2016. Polls and Electoral College maps were frequently used to demoralize Trump voters by presenting the false impression that Trump had no way to win the election. Mainstream media regularly used some of the most unreliable and demographically unbalanced polls as psyops against Trump. One of the most historically accurate political polls, the *USC Dornsife/Los Angeles Times "Daybreak"* poll, which called both of Obama's elections *correctly*, consistently showed Trump in a range between even to seven percent ahead among likely voters who were asked, *"Who would you vote for?"* throughout September and October. Other less accurate and purposely skewed polls, showed Hillary ahead, which was accomplished by oversampling Democrats by ten to fifteen points. One such poll showed Hillary ahead by thirteen points on the same day the *LA Times* poll had Trump up by three.

"Oversampling" simply means putting more Democrats into a poll than are likely to vote in a given election. For example, late in October, 2016, an *ABC News* poll had Hillary Clinton leading Donald Trump by twelve points. Not reported in the headline was that nine percent more Democrats than Republicans were questioned by the polltakers. Playing fast and loose with polls is a common Democrat-media psyops tactic. In an email released by Wikileaks, Democrat operative Tom Matzzie admitted the purposeful use of oversampling when he wrote, "I want to get your people to recommend oversamples for our polling before we start in February ... I want to get this all compiled into one set of recommendations, so we can maximize what we get out of our media polling."

During the campaign, the mainstream media regularly relied upon polling conducted by Hart Research Associates/Public Opinion Strategies, which frequently had Hillary up by double digits over Trump. Hart Research was led by

Geoff Garin, who at the same time was working for Hillary's campaign and running a SuperPAC called PrioritiesUSA that dumped millions into the firm. Simply put, Hillary paid for her own poll results and the entire mainstream media reported them as fact.

Many other psyops were coordinated between Hillary and the media and were later exposed in emails released by Wikileaks:

1. Clinton Staff hosts private "off-the-record cocktail party" with thirty-eight "influential" reporters, journalists, editors, and anchors, from sixteen different mainstream media outlets, including CNN, NBC, CBS, NYT, and MSNBC, with the stated goal of "framing the race."

2. CNN contributor and DNC Chairman Donna Brazile leaked the questions in CNN's Town Hall broadcast to Hillary Clinton's staff prior to the debate.

3. Clinton campaign and *The New York Times* coordinating attack strategy against Trump.

4. Glenn Thrush, POLITICO's chief political correspondent and senior staff writer for *POLITICO Magazine*, sent Clinton Campaign Manager, John Podesta, an article for his approval. He wrote, "Please don't share or tell anyone I did this. Tell me if I f***ed up anything."

5. Huffington Post contributor Frank Islam wrote to John Podesta in an email titled, "My blogs in the Huffington Post." He assured Hillary Clinton's campaign manager,

"I am committed to make sure she is elected the next president…. Please let me know if I can be of any service to you."

6. A Clinton staffer openly described placing a story with POLITICO and *The New York Times*. He wrote about how he had placed "a story with a friendly journalist," and claimed, "we have a very good relationship with Maggie Haberman of POLITICO," and said, "we should shape likely leaks in the best light for HRC."

7. Clinton Campaign Manager John Podesta received drafts of articles written for *The New York Times* before they were published.

8. Hillary Clinton's staff colluded with *The New York Times* and *The Wall Street Journal* in order to present Hillary's economic policies in a "progressive" light.

9. A CNBC panelist asked Clinton Campaign Manager John Podesta what to ask Donald Trump when Trump called in for a scheduled interview.

10. Hillary Clinton's staff were observed to be able to influence the release times of *Associated Press* articles.

Perhaps one of the most demoralizing psyops to Trump supporters was performed by Fox News. Although they are often considered to be the conservative cable news network, Fox News is controlled opposition. "Controlled opposition" is when a deliberate attempt is made to create an opposing effort to an existing friendly power base or to obtain control of the opposition to one's own efforts. In this case, Fox News portrays itself as the "conservative alternative" to mainstream news, but, in reality, it is merely a facet of the mainstream news itself. Fox News' role is to bring in voters who identify as Republican and create the illusion of a free dialogue and alternative reporting, while only engaging with a specific set of issues defined to be safe by liberals.

Fox News uses hosts like Sean Hannity, and now Tucker Carlson, who have big enough platforms to avoid being co-opted, to bring in conservatives and Republicans, but then throws false narratives and abject lies at them in order to demoralize the Trump supporters. No Fox News host was worse during the 2016 campaign than the now thoroughly discredited Megyn Kelly, who was fired from the network after viewers abandoned her due to her transparent assaults on Trump and Trump supporters. It should come as no surprise, then, that Fox News' parent corporation, News Corp, donated $3,002,926 to Bill and Hillary Clinton in their various political campaigns over the years. In addition, the News Corporation Foundation is listed on the Clinton Foundation website as a donor between the $500,001 and $1,000,000 levels. Its owner, Rupert Murdoch, is also listed as a Clinton Foundation donor between the $1,000,001 and $5,000,000 levels.

Had Donald Trump and Hillary Clinton run for President in 1992, there is no question that Hillary Clinton would have won, given the absolute monopoly the mainstream media held over the dissemination of information at that time. However, in 2016, social media and the Internet have democratized information, which has allowed individual content creators to spread news to others throughout the world. It has also allowed independent media organizations to rise, such as *Infowars, Breitbart, Rebel Media, Drudge Report, FreeDomainRadio, The Daily Caller,* and *The Rubin Report.* These outlets routinely challenge the narratives and tropes propagated by the mainstream media and, in return, they are routinely derided and no-platformed by the media and the technology giants in an attempt to keep the media's massive, fine-tuned psyop running smoothly.

But whether it runs smoothly or not, it is fake news. Don't fall for it.

Chapter 4

The Tyranny of Labels

Never forget what you are, for surely the world will not. Make it your strength. Then it can never be your weakness.

—Tyrion Lannister

One often-used tactic of the media Left could be called the "tyranny of labels." It is the mischaracterization of a group or individual described through a partisan and adversarial lens. Is President Trump a white racist or an American nationalist? Is he a conspiracy theorist or a master persuader? In 2018, the truth depends on what side of the political aisle you stand. The media often seeks to taint, prejudge, and discredit those who disagree with them by applying an editorialized label to them, rather than accurately reporting a person's position.

This was recently evidenced in the media coverage of University of Toronto professor, Jordan Peterson. Many media outlets that tout their supposed objectivity began referring to him as the "Controversial Professor Jordan Peterson." However, upon looking into the matter, I can confirm that no such position as Controversial Professor exists at the University of Toronto. The only position Jordan Peterson holds is Professor of Psychology, a position he has held for twenty years. Prior to that, he was an Associate Professor of Psychology at Harvard University. To the dishonest leftist media, none of this factual information matters. What matters to them is portraying him as a figure of the right and, therefore, someone who must be immediately discredited before anyone hears a word he has to say. *The Chronicle of Higher Education* refers to him as "polarizing." *Slate* calls him an "alt-right hero." *The Independent* calls him a "provocateur." All of these phrases are inaccurate mischaracterizations or editorial opinions, dressed up and presented as fact in news reporting.

The following is a list of phrases often employed by the media in order to mischaracterize and discredit anyone with whom they do not agree, especially supporters of President Trump. If you see these phrases employed, you should immediately understand that you are reading hyperpartisan and biased opinion, not the objective and honest reporting of straightforward facts:

- White supremacist

- Nazi

- Conspiracy theorist

- Russian-linked

- Racist

- Sexist

- Alt-right

- Far-right

- Anti-Semitic

- Misinformation

- Disinformation

- Doxxer

- Harasser

- Hoaxer

- Liar

- Peddler

- Troll

- Fake news

- Moneygrubbing

- Fraud

These frequent mischaracterizations are dangerous, because they remove credibility from the labels themselves, which renders them unable to accurately portray those groups that purvey hateful or bigoted beliefs, such as genuine white supremacists. In truth, Trump supporters and nationalists are a center-right coalition, often influenced by the Christian religion. Wanting to reform immigration laws does not make someone a Nazi any more than calling for increased taxes makes someone a Bolshevik. Questioning the legitimacy of official government and party documents does not make someone a "conspiracy theorist" any more than being a whistleblower calling for corporate accountability does. Being a Trump supporter does not mean someone is "Russian-linked" no matter how many times the Atlantic Council neocons declare that to be the case.

The following is a second list of more accurate labels for Trump supporters and members of the New Media. While these phrases may not be preferred by those in the media Left, if you see them, they indicate the writer, despite his own political leanings, is making an attempt to be objective in his reporting:

- Nationalist

- Trump supporter

- Pro-Trump

- New Right

- Right-wing

- Conservative

- Patriot Movement

- Muckraker

- Whistleblower

- Activist

- Filmmaker

- Media Critic

- Writer

- Blogger

- Author

As a final example of the media's persistent bias, here is one phrase I have never seen the media utilize in reference to me—although it's the first line of my bio, completely accurate, and correctly describes my background, as well as my years dedicated to serving the United States of America:

"*Veteran Navy Intelligence Officer.*"

Let that sink in.

Chapter 5

Denial and Deception

Rhaegar fought valiantly, Rhaegar fought nobly, Rhaegar fought honorably. And Rhaegar died.

—Jorah Mormont

One of the major problems in any discussion of deception is the ambiguity of the term and the wide variety of meanings that different people assign to it. Some people use the term broadly, using it to refer to political or military strategies that conceal their true goals, active propaganda measures, policy statements by national leaders that conceal or misrepresent information in order to gain an advantage over rivals, or even measures taken to limit public knowledge of operations. By this definition, deception is pervasive in politics.

On the other hand, some people use the term "deception" more narrowly in reference to a specific set of activities. They make a sharp distinction between broad perception management activities aimed at specific policymakers and the public, and disinformation that is passed through controlled intelligence channels, such as double agents or compromised technical intelligence collection systems for the purpose of deceiving those analysts on the other side. These people would argue that only the latter sorts of activities are properly referred to as "deception."

Regardless, the word "deception" contains multiple meanings, many of which are legitimate, depending on the circumstances. The issue isn't which usage of the term is, or should be, correct, but rather, how we can communicate most effectively about any important subject in order to manage perceptions and achieve our goals. Perception management refers to activities aimed at leaders, influencers, and the public to influence how they perceive an action, an individual, or a situation. Such activities include self-serving or deceptive statements by leaders, the covert placement of articles in media, forgeries, the use of public influence agents, and broadcasting propaganda through front groups and the media.

In a discussion of perception management, its probable impact needs consideration: *What is the impact of this deception on adversary leaders? Does it influence their operatives? Does it modify the information they believe to be true? And should adversary operatives or some other element of the adversary coalition play a more active role in combating the impact of perception management on adversary leaders?*

The CIA defines deception as, "an action or set of coordinated actions intended to mislead through the creation or perpetuation of false perceptions with the objective to induce the opponent to act, or react, in a way prejudicial to his interests." The purpose of deception is to cause an adversary to act in a way that is not in his best interest, without the adversary realizing what was done to him and, more importantly, who did it.

CIA-defined denial includes the routine operational security known as OPSEC, such as practiced by military forces. It also includes withholding information that is deemed sensitive at the time. Denial, strictly speaking, is not deception, but denial activities are usually part of any major deception operation. Denial measures are generally intended to promote uncertainties and confuse assessments, whereas deception is intended to lead an opponent towards erroneous conclusions. Therefore, denial tends to involve more passive measures while deception is usually more active.

As a term, "deception" carries a lot of baggage. Nobody wants to admit that his judgment is flawed or that he's been misled by undetected deception. Being deceived suggests we are naïve or have not devoted significant time and energy to understanding the problem. But it is important to grasp that deception is designed to create a component of ambiguity that renders your judgment less effective. Deception is designed to affect the judgment of adversary operatives, especially as it concerns their analysis of your goals. In short, deception helps you to achieve your goals by confusing your adversaries about what they truly are.

Disinformation is best described as the dissemination of false, half-true, and misleading information. Disinformation is often combined with truthful information and is designed to achieve a specific objective. Disinformation is similar to propaganda, but not synonymous with it. Propaganda is overtly aimed at a mass audience, either foreign or domestic, and it is not necessarily deceptive. In contrast, disinformation is aimed only at specific targets, is deliberately deceptive, and is usually utilized in a covert manner.

Strategic deception involves large-scale deception programs designed to achieve major national objectives. Such a program involves multiple deception plans and a wide array of deceptive techniques. One of the greatest examples of strategic deception is the deception operations carried out by the allies leading up to the Normandy landings in 1944. These deception operations tricked the Germans into thinking that Calais was the mainland landing area rather than Normandy. They achieved this objective through the use of fake uniforms, fake communications, fake documents, and even the death of a fake soldier.

The Normandy strategic deception campaign was so successful that it was not until several days after the Allied landings that the German High Command realized that Normandy was, in fact, the primary invasion site.

Deception operations successfully target multiple cognitive biases that all humans exhibit to varying degrees. Some of these include biases and estimating probabilities, availability bias, anchoring bias, overconfidence bias, biases in evaluating of evidence, oversensitivity to consistency, absence of evidence, persistence of impressions based on discredited evidence, the perception of causality, casual explanations, and internal-versus-external causes of behavior. Because people tend to cling to their beliefs, they tend to see patterns where none actually exist. They also tend to assume that the simplest solution is the correct one, tend to trust the last thing they heard, and dislike having their biases challenged. Deception operations take advantage of all these tendencies.

Psychologists argue that individuals are most likely to follow their predispositions when they are relaxed or when they are very tense. In the first case, facing no urgency to make a decision, individuals see no disadvantage in going along with their original predispositions. On the other hand, when pressed to make important decisions in a hurry, people tend to fall prey to what they subconsciously choose to see. In this state, moderate tension, or vigilance responses, are elicited that overcome predispositions and confirmation bias. Individuals are then more open-minded as they seek out information to make a rational decision.

This dichotomy means that those intending to change a target's beliefs through deception should confront a target with the need to make an important decision, while avoiding placing the subject in a crisis situation. In Operation Mincemeat, the British presented the Germans with a variety of clues suggesting that Sardinia would be invaded some time in the coming months, but not any time soon. Hitler and his intelligence officers were given excuses to doubt their previous expectations about an Allied invasion of Sicily. They were given time to reassess the situation and put together an alternative scenario incorporating Sardinia. Had the British pushed the Germans into a crisis decision-making mode, the Germans probably would not have shifted their forces in the way the deceiving British intended.

Democracies mostly employ denial and deception in wartime, but they are quite capable of utilizing deception in peacetime as well. From the Revolutionary War campaign at Yorktown to the D-Day landings in World War II and the famous feint of a Marine amphibious assault during the Gulf War, U.S. history is full of examples in which deception was used to the U.S. military's advantage. Throughout the 20ᵗʰ century, Great Britain and other democracies also showed themselves to be effective at using deception in both war and peace. For example, Israel and India's programs to develop nuclear weapons benefited from sophisticated denial-and-deception campaigns. Americans, however, are often unaware of the way in which foreign democracies waged these campaigns against them.

In contrast to democracies, authoritarian and totalitarian regimes tend to utilize denial and deception as a regular instrument of governance. This increases their reliance on utilizing similar tactics for foreign policy and defense. Especially disturbing is the tendency of authoritarian and totalitarian regimes to use denial and deception in the support of initiating hostilities at the beginning of a war. One example is the very sophisticated denial-and-deception campaign leading up to Japan's attack on the United States in December, 1941.

Non-state actors regularly utilize denial and deception, far more than anyone else on the planet. Transnational businesses, criminal syndicates, revolutionary organizations, terrorists, and other groups pursuing illegal objectives must seek cover in order to operate effectively. For criminals, rebels, and terrorists, denial and deception often becomes their *raison d'être*. The shadowy world of the terrorist or the criminal is an alternative reality rather than a short-term solution to achieve limited objectives. The terrorist flourishes in the hidden world created by denial, while the gunman uses both denial and deception to enter the world of legitimate power. The clandestine underground is a way of life as well as a strategic instrument for highly illegal organizations. For clandestine groups, creating a parallel world offers a safe haven and enhances the life of the committed member. Of course, these alternate realities don't come without risks.

The habitual use of deception and denial are visible in criminal cartels that seek public respect, power, and money, in terrorist organizations that seek to change the direction of history through violent action, and in radical religious cults. Through the use of denial and deception, even the most murderous cult, such as the People's Temple or Aum Shinrikyo, may be perceived as benign by outsiders. Consider how Islamic extremists in the United States were generally ignored prior to the 1993 attack on New York City's World Trade Center.

Denial and deception tactics are used by organizations around the world, by the mainstream media, by terrorists, by political parties, and by individuals. These tools must be studied and understood by anyone operating in the 4D warfare space. Information warfare is replete with thousands of examples of successful denial and deception. Deception may be overcome, but doing so relies on the ability of the individual to see it for what it is. In general, it is wise to regard any new piece of information as potential deception.

Chapter 6

The Maoist Cultural Revolution of America

Oh, my sweet summer child.

—Old Nan

Antifa is a failed psyop.

Antifa was intended to start a narrative that "Trump creates violence." In reality, thanks to New Media and the efforts of countless thousands, that narrative has been replaced by the observable truth that, "the Left is violent."

Let's dive deeper, shall we?

A soft cultural revolution is happening in the United States. The end state goal of these revolutionaries is socialism. In many ways, their tactics and concepts are similar to the Chinese Cultural Revolution under Chairman Mao. Chairman Mao destroyed Chinese culture. He tore down statues, tortured individuals, and killed anyone who stood in his way. Everyone who challenged—or even threatened to challenge—the rule of the supreme communist dictator was destroyed.

The Chinese communist and cultural revolution lasted for ten years, from 1966 to 1976. The Holocaust Memorial Museum estimates the death toll of that period between five and ten million. During that time, communist revolutionaries shut down nearly every school and institution of higher learning in the country. They destroyed ancient Chinese culture. They destroyed everything that Chairman Mao stood against because he saw the destruction of the past as the only way to permit what he considered to be progress toward the future. Chairman Mao's destruction of Chinese culture is akin to what the Alt-Left is doing today. They're attacking our culture and the American way of life.

Ancient Chinese history was attacked, destroyed, and systematically erased from modern China. Relics, paintings and statues were smashed. Old books were burned to ashes. This was not just a symptom of the Communist revolution, it was their specific and stated objective. Not a flaw, but a design! Statues were destroyed, temples were burned, gravesites were smashed and even the language itself was transformed. For example, the great city of Peking became Beijing. Why did they do this? They did it to facilitate their social engineering program on the Chinese people.

The primary instrument utilized by Mao in his anti-cultural campaign was the Red Guards. The Red Guards were an organization of Chinese youth that Chairman Mao set up to be his unquestionably loyal soldiers in the streets. They reported directly to him. He didn't trust the police and the military to do exactly what he wanted to the letter, so he bypassed them by creating a paramilitary group composed primarily of students. Chairman Mao broadcast the extremist manifesto of the Red Guards on national radio and had it printed in the official Communist Party newspapers and propaganda releases. Red Guard factions sprouted up around the country, comprised of extremist youth who were unfailingly loyal to Chairman Mao, their flames of extremism fanned by his public pronouncements.

The Red Guards began to destroy temples, ancient cities and gravesites. They even killed people who spoke out against their actions. An entire generation was lost to madness and Mao made it happen. He did everything he could do to make them violent. He did everything he could do to inspire the youth to attack regular people in the streets and in their homes.

Does this sound similar to what you're seeing today? This is the actual history of what happened in China from the 1960s into the 1970s. The insanity only ended with the death of Chairman Mao. Some scholars refer to the Chinese Cultural Revolution as state terrorism. Not only did the cultural revolution greatly increase the level of violence throughout China, the violence took place both with the Red Guards and without them.

The most vicious example of the factional fighting that took place occurred in the southern province of Guangxi during the summer of 1968. One provincial faction refused to recognize the authority of Mao's point man, General Wei Guoqing, who had helped direct the climactic battle against the French at Dien Bien Phu in Vietnam in 1954. Wei was determined to use any degree of force to crush his opponents. This involved not only using machine guns, mortars, and artillery, but also inciting gruesome murders of large numbers of people designated by the regime as class enemies. The boss of the Binyang County, an Army officer told his attendants, "I'm now going to reveal the bottom line to you in this campaign. We are going to put to death one-third or a quarter of the class enemies by bludgeoning or stoning."

It was a straightforward terror campaign as killing by simple shooting was considered insufficiently frightening to the population.

This was 1968. Fifty years later, Antifa was attacking police in Boston with stones and urine. This has all happened before. The Cultural Revolution is one of the most insane things that happened to one of the largest groups of people in the entire world. It didn't happen that long ago, but for some reason there are no movies about it, there are very few books about it, historians don't teach about it, and no one on the History Channel is talking about it. Due to the significant Chinese investments in Hollywood, no mainstream media outlets or Hollywood studios ever address the Maoist Cultural Revolution.

The Red Guards educated the masses through stoning and killings over a period of 11 days after the order was given. Starting on July 26, 1968, 3,681 people in Binyang County were beaten to death. The ghastly killing during the Cultural Revolution ultimately claimed 100,000 lives in the province. The authorities staged what they called, "model demonstrations of killing," to show people how to apply maximum cruelty and, in some cases, the police even supervised the killings.

In that cruel atmosphere, supply lines were cut off, leading to widespread starvation. Cannibalism broke out in many parts of the province. The best-known example took place in the county of Wu Chuah, where a post-Mao official investigation was promptly halted in 1983 and its findings were suppressed after seventy-six victims were identified. The practice of cannibalism started with the Maoist staple of denunciation rallies. Victims were slaughtered immediately afterwards, and the choice parts of their bodies—hearts, livers, and sexual organs—were often removed before the victims were dead and cooked on the spot to be eaten in what were openly called, "human flesh banquets." This was all supervised and sponsored by the Communist government under Chairman Mao.

Guangxi is a region with some of the most picturesque landscapes in China. Exquisite hills rise and fall over crystal-clear waters in which the reflected peaks look as real as they do above. It was against these heavenly double silhouettes by the rivers that the human flesh banquets were served. An 86-year-old peasant slit open the chest of a boy in broad daylight. The child's only crime was being the son of a rich landlord. People had no trouble finding justifications for these actions in Mao's words. "Yes, I killed him," the man later told an investigative writer. "The person I killed is a class enemy, you see. I make a revolution and my heart is red. Didn't Chairman Mao say, 'It's either I kill them, or they kill us?' You die, I live. This is class struggle."

In 1968, state-sponsored killings peaked in every province. That year was dominated by a mammoth campaign called, "Sort Out Class Ranks." The aim was to inventory every single class enemy in the entire population and to impose various punishments on them, up to and including execution. All the victims from before and during the Cultural Revolution were dragged out and persecuted again. In addition, the regime set out to uncover new enemies by scrutinizing the history and conduct of every adult in the nation. Consider how they were scrutinizing the conduct of every adult in the nation. Think about that the next time you open up Google or Facebook and are asked if you want to share your data and share your location. Do you really want to share your personal data when you know about what can happen when they later decide to scrutinize your history? The number of people labeled "official outcasts" ran to twenty-three million.

People stopped going to work. The economy was seriously interrupted. Industries were shuttered in order to force people to engage in what were called, "struggle sessions." Even in the totalitarian state, an element of anarchy crept in. One of the Party members gave Mao's travel schedule to a student who fancied himself a detective. He was able to trail Mao covertly around the country. Although both the student and the Party member were soon discovered and arrested, such a complete lapse in security had never before taken place.

The Cultural Revolution was sick and disgusting and we must not let something similar happen in our country. The Great Purge killed millions of people. Learning from their fathers and friends that Mao was encouraging violence, the young Red Guards immediately embarked on atrocities. The first known death by torture took place on August 5, in a Beijing girls' school packed with high officials' children. The headmistress, a fifty-year-old mother of four, was kicked and trampled by girls. Boiling water was poured on her. She was ordered to carry heavy bricks back and forth and as she stumbled past, she was thrashed with leather Army belts with brass buckles and with wooden sticks studded with nails. She soon collapsed and died. Afterwards, leading activists reported to the new authority. They were not told to stop—a tacit approval for them to carry on. This is what they're doing right now. They're whipping up the youth, whipping up those who don't have the mental capacity to understand at their age. This is a repeat of history happening right in front of us, as if I'm reading from a history book. I've read many books about Mao, Stalin, Hitler and what happened before. You guys need to understand these things. I read this stuff. I can even speak Chinese fluently. I've dug into history, because we cannot allow this to happen in America.

Chairman Mao said it straight up. He said, "Political power grows from the barrel of a gun." He knew it. He knew exactly how to rile up his people. He riled up the Red Guards. He riled them up to burn American flags like the one that's right behind me. It's a flag that was burned by Antifa during the 2016 Democratic National Convention. They are trying to start Civil War II by starting a cultural revolution within our country on Marxist/Maoist terms. What Chairman Mao did was radicalize the youth to the point where they could commit violence against authorities, against their parents, against their leaders, against their own families and against their own mothers and fathers. He radicalized the youth to the point where violence didn't matter. Sure, the elderly also got involved—a lot of people got involved—but radicalizing the youth is a really big part of this evil. You had students in schools killing their own principals.

Suicides skyrocketed during Chairman Mao's Cultural Revolution because people were overcome with fear. Had they ever done anything, or said anything, or spoken out against Chairman Mao? Had they ever said anything against communism or what was going on in their country that somebody might remember? If you were labeled "right-wing" during that time, you were *dead*. If you were labeled "right-wing" during the cultural Revolution, it didn't matter what you said—it didn't matter what your evidence was—it didn't matter what your issues were... you were dead. You were just straight-up *dead*. You were tortured, and you were put in front of a crowd— including your own family—then you would be made to apologize and repudiate yourself in front of all those people. This was what took place at these "struggle sessions." You would be put in front of them and you would be killed. You would be shot right in front of everyone, and then they would make your parents or your family pay for the bullets. They called it the "bullet tax" at the time. You need to understand that this stuff that the left is riling up is demonic and it is disgusting. It is absolutely horrific that this is where they are pushing us.

We saw CNN during the summer of 2017 giving Antifa a free pass. Even *endorsing* Antifa. When CNN saw Antifa, they compared them to the World War II soldiers who fought at Normandy. That's not what's going on. We're not at war right now. There is no war going on within the United States. The United States isn't even in a declared war now. They are trying to impose a soft cultural revolution on us, the same way that Chairman Mao imposed his extreme cultural revolution in China. If that happens, I pray for our country. If that happens, you had better be ready. Read about it. Read about the Chinese Cultural Revolution. This is history. This *happened*. This is real. It happened forty-five years ago and Antifa is flying the same red flags today. Antifa is holding the flags today that Chairman Mao loved to see his Red Guards flying.

Chairman Mao would be proud of Antifa.

Chapter 7

Fake Friends, Fake Enemies

Sellswords put gold before honor.

—Illyrio Mopatis

Another example of a failed psyop narrative by the media is how they've used fake conservatives to attack real ones.

One of the mainstream media's favorite tactics is to portray someone who is a liberal as a Republican and then use them to attack people on the right. This tactic is regularly used against President Trump. One of the reasons they do this is because they believe that by labeling someone as a Republican, or using someone who, in the past, had been labeled as a Republican, gives their line of attack on another Republican more credibility. Like many of the Left's tactics, this is something that was done throughout communist countries.

By featuring someone seen as on their "side," the media sends the viewer a message that this person has credibility to talk about these issues, because they are on the same team. This is similar to when the Left quotes the Bible in the context of a debate about illegal immigration or border security. The Left could not care less about the Bible or Christianity, but they use the tactic to defeat conservative arguments by portraying conservatives as entirely Christian. While it is true that there are many conservative Christians—myself being one—it is also true that there are Jewish conservatives, there are Muslim conservatives, and there are Buddhist conservatives. It is also true that there are many Christians who are Democrats.

Yet CNN, nonetheless, continues to portray many liberals as Republicans and as conservatives in order to attack and impugn other Republicans and conservatives. One of the greatest examples of this was CNN commentator, Ana Navarro. Ana did not appreciate it when we exposed her in 2017—dubbing it, #AnaGate.

The media lost their minds over #AnaGate. *Media Matters* attacked me, claiming it was a smear campaign organized by Posobiec and Hannity against Ana Navarro. *A smear campaign from the right-wing conspiracy theory machine.* It was a vast right-wing conspiracy! Then they admitted that Posobiec researched publicly available information. What they were really saying was that we told the truth—they just didn't *like* it. I wrote the story of #AnaGate on August 24, along with the incredible Stephen Chretien, and the great Roger Stone. We looked into Ana Navarro's records. We looked into her donations, which you can find at FEC.gov. Anyone can do this, but apparently nobody thought to before I did. Nobody thought to get into Ana Navarro and #AnaGate before Jack Posobiec. Ana went around calling herself a "Republican," even though she donated $20,000 of her own money to the Democrat Party. That was the first red flag. The second was that she organized three—count them—*three* fundraisers for Sen. Bob Menendez when he was indicted for corruption charges. She donated to him three times, at a time when the *New York*

Daily News—which is not a Republican nor right-wing/right-leaning publication, whatsoever—was saying that prosecutors were going after Democrat Sen. Robert Menendez for having sex with underage hookers in the Dominican Republic. This was someone Ana mentioned in a tweet, writing, "I've known Menendez +20 yrs. He's tough, smart, resolute. Not easy to intimidate. Not likely to break. Will give prosecutors hell of a fight." Ana Navarro also said that "if the DOJ indicts Menendez they better have an airtight case. He's tough Hudson County bareknuckle fighter not type that scares easily." That's Ana Navarro. Those tweets have not aged well.

Since I conducted my initial research, other great organizations have gone out there. *LifeZette* has probably done the best analysis of this, after me. Four days after my article, Jim Stinson at *LifeZette* conducted a full analysis and found that over $20,000 went from this "Republican consultant" to the Democrat party from the "Republican" Navarro. Roger Stone, who we all know is a Republican operative and a consultant, says that CNN should be sued for having labeled her a "Republican strategist" for all these years. Not only has Ana Navarro donated and held fundraisers for indicted Democrat Sen. Bob Menendez, Navarro has even gone so far as to donate to Debbie Wasserman Schultz, the chair of the Democrat National Committee, who we all know was embroiled in the indictment of the IT staffers that she formally hired, that have ties to Pakistani intelligence, known as the, "Awan brothers." She's also friends with Erica Gutierrez. She's also friends with a lot of dirty people. These guys are not mainstream Republicans. In fact, they are hard-left Democrats. Ana Navarro admits, by the way, that her father was a member of the CIA-sponsored group, the Contras, in Nicaragua. $20,000 in donations to Democrats. If you're on CNN with Navarro and happen to find yourself in a debate with her, simply say, "Ana, why do you go around calling yourself a 'Republican strategist' when, number one, you've never offered strategic consultation to Republicans? And, number two, why do you donate to Democrats when you're a Republican?" Maybe Ana Navarro is trying to play 4D chess? Maybe Ana Navarro thinks giving $20,000 to Democrats is going to help Republicans? If only I had a crystal ball or some way to find out how it is, exactly, that giving $20,000 to Democrats helps the Republicans. By the way, the original election of Bob Menendez gave the Senate to the Democrat Party in 2006. I was working in Republican politics and had connections to the Senate in 2006. So, why are we not going to get any information about this from Ana Navarro? Why is she going around running her mouth like she's a Republican? She's a Democrat! With Donald Trump, we all know that he has donated to Democrats in the past. He has been completely open about it and has nothing to hide. He admits that giving to both sides was part of being a businessman. He didn't lie to anyone nor claim it didn't happen. He simply said, *that is what I am doing, this is who I am, I admit it.* So, Ana, why are you running around calling yourself a "Republican strategist?" Why can't you be clean with us? Why can't you simply tell us the truth about who you are? Why are you gaslighting your own viewers?

In August of 2017, Navarro and Republican Representative Steve Montenegro were on CNN, debating Trump's pardon of Sheriff Joe Arpaio, when Montenegro said to her, "You're a Republican, but you're also a liberal. We're talking about a narrative that tries to pin conservatives and Republicans as racists."

Navarro began screaming. "Why am I a liberal?! Because I stand up for my community? Why am I a liberal? Because I want to defend the DREAM Act kids? Why am I a liberal? Because I don't forget that I am an immigrant, and I am Hispanic, and I have a Latin accent when I speak English?!" She angrily continued, "Why am I liberal? Because I believe in gay rights?" She also added, "And, yes, I voted for Hillary Clinton."

Chris Cuomo is a Democrat activist, and Jake Tapper won't tell you the fact that they're Democrat activists. Ana Navarro couldn't win the argument so she screamed and shouted down her opponents while grasping at straws. She was triggered. All I did was go and look up some basic facts about Ana Navarro. Anyone could have gone to FEC.gov and done it.

Chapter 8

The Great Russian Conspiracy Theory

Why cling to these false gods?

—Melisandre

There has been no single greater evidence of a rank conspiracy theory being thrust upon the American people than The Great Russian Conspiracy. Beginning in late 2016, and dominating headlines up until now, the theory is that Russia and its intelligence services conspired with Donald Trump to sway the 2016 election. Thousands of articles, thousands of hours of television, and hundreds of hours of testimony have been dedicated to the furtherance of this psychological operation—so much so that the Department of Justice even went as far as to appoint a special prosecutor named Robert Mueller to look into the matter.

At the time of this writing, there has been no evidence given to demonstrate a link between Donald Trump's campaign for president and the Russian state. Furthermore, there has been no evidence provided that the Russian state altered the outcome of the United States presidential election. The FBI investigation has been running for over a year and a half and millions of taxpayer dollars have been spent in the effort. Depending on the source, the investigation may have begun as far back as July 2016 or even early 2015. Despite no evidence being provided in all of that time, the mainstream media continues reporting breathlessly on any new update to this fictional plotline.

The Russia conspiracy theory has all the hallmarks of a deception psyop. It plays into the cognitive dissonance of disaffected liberals and establishment voters, as well as elites who were reassured for *two years* that there was *no way Donald Trump could ever win the presidency.* To them, this was an aberration of history itself. They all read industrial media articles from the likes of *The New York Times* and *The Huffington Post* that assuaged their fears and reported unequivocally that there was no possibility that Donald Trump would win. Despite numerous reputations of evidence, and countless retracted articles and apologies, no mainstream publication nor establishment politician has simply stepped forward to admit that the entire thing was built on a foundation of lies and that Americans need to accept the fact that Trump won.

In fact, some media even go so far as to report on the Russia conspiracy theory as established fact. Articles are written that talk about the Trump campaign's connection to Russia, or Russian interference in the U.S. election, or Russian connections to Wikileaks, or Russia hacking the DNC—as if those things were not highly controversial and dubious statements. These reports have no credibility nor integrity. It's one thing to report a partisan disagreement and give both sides of that disagreement, but in the world of the Russia conspiracy theory, everything the Democrats say is taken at face value and everything that Trump supporters say is looked at with suspicion—after all, they are Russian agents, right?

The Democrats have pinned their political futures on the Russia conspiracy theory as some sort of Hail Mary. However, it risks a large backlash if it fails to grant their fervent wish to bring down the president. The Democrats have no control over nationwide government—they have no control over most state governments and, for the most part, only represent liberal bicoastal enclaves. Though those enclaves are some of the richest and most well-defended territories of the United States, the fact remains that the Democrats are now a regional party. Instead of reforming their standing, they decided to lash out at their opponents through a campaign of conspiracy theorizing and fever-pitch sensationalism by their toadies in the industrial media.

Due to the paralysis imposed upon his administration by the Russia conspiracy theory, the president now has great difficulty pushing forward major foreign policy proposals and reforms. He is also unable to push forward his legislative agenda with half of the Congress declaring him to be some sort of Manchurian candidate that needs to be removed from office for reasons of national security. You have to admit, the Russians—and every intelligence service around the world—are probably loving this, because the United States has now been taken out of action around the world, and others are left with nearly a free hand, since the president of the United States is preoccupied battling a crisis that exists only in the minds of Democrats.

At this point, U.S. intelligence agencies have absolutely destroyed their credibility. The CIA, the DNI, and the FBI have engaged in partisan politics after an election they clearly wish had gone the other way and have thrown in with a conspiracy theory based on smoke and mirrors rather than hard fact. Their half-baked assessments and blatant partisanship have ruined the public image of the intelligence community for at least a generation. Now the public is learning that members of the intelligence agencies worked with the Democrat party and the biased industrial media to report "facts" based on a Democrat opposition research dossier, which has never been verified and is apparently the publication of a freelancer working in Europe and Russian intelligence sources. Yes, you read that correctly: *Russian intel sources.* Steele claimed he based his dossier on information shared by Russian agents. There is every indication that these statements are traditional Russian disinformation designed to create precisely the situation which now exists within the United States.

If it turned out to be true that the Russia investigation and the conspiracy theory of Russian collusion with Trump was actually a psyop perpetrated on the Left and U.S. intelligence services by the Russian state, it may go down in history as one of the greatest psyops of all time. From a few simple statements, to a single source in Europe, an entire conspiracy theory was born, entrapping nearly the entire U.S. counterintelligence apparatus, the entire U.S. industrial media, half of the political process in the United States, and ultimately the president of the United States himself. Somewhere, Putin is laughing at all of us right now.

Chapter 9

Russian 4D Warfare in Crimea

It is one thing to be clever and another to be wise.

—Catelyn Stark

Russia has been a nonstop topic since the election of Trump, yet Russia's skill with information was well-known to the international community long before the recent controversy. Whether or not Russia was involved in the U.S. election is a matter that is still under intense debate, though there is little evidence that there was any direct connection between the Russian state and the Donald Trump campaign. Yet we do know that Russia has employed information warfare against their adversaries for many years. Russia has stated that its information warfare goal against the United States is strategic deterrence—meaning its goal within the United States is not to pick winners and losers, but to create a state of chaos within the U.S. political system so that no one party nor side can take full power. The goal is to get everyone fighting each other so much that the United States cannot extend its reach and its influence around the world in international affairs. Sounds like 2018, doesn't it?

Supposed election meddling aside, there is a much better example of Russian information warfare the mainstream media seems to have completely forgotten: Crimea. Immediately following the impeachment of Ukrainian President Yanukovych in 2014, Russia began agitating for influence over Crimea. Russia maintains a military base there at Sevastopol, a major naval port on the Black Sea, and would not readily accept giving it up. Russia considered President Yanukovych's impeachment as a coup, and painted the backers of the coup as Nazis influenced by the West. Russia then stated that it had a moral duty to protect the ethnic Russians living in Crimea and eastern Ukraine. Russia argued that the basic rights of ethnic Russians were being violated, and since the West—and, specifically, the CIA—was responsible for the coup in Ukraine, Russia had to intervene to protect their kin. Russia views Ukraine as a line that cannot be crossed and decided to act in order to preserve their sovereignty and sphere of influence over the region, with Russian military interests particularly in mind. Russia's Black Sea fleet has been headquartered at Crimea for over two hundred and fifty years. Russia also wanted to show that when they draw a line in the sand, they will not allow it to be crossed by the West, regardless of the circumstances.

There were essentially three tiers to Russia's information warfare strategy in Ukraine: Tier 1 was that controlling the territory resulted in sovereignty. The stunted reaction of Barack Obama and his European Union allies clearly indicated that this was successful. Tier 2 was backing up every single Russian action through a legal act. Regardless of the merits of these legal acts, every single step that Russia took was supported through a form of legislation or a writ sent from the higher government. In this way, they were able to build a legal case that their actions in the annexation of Crimea were not illegal. Finally, Tier 3 was popular support. Immediately after the annexation of Crimea, Russia held a referendum within the Peninsula, which it handily won, demonstrating that Crimeans wanted to be part of Russia, not Ukraine.

What Russia did was use nearly all of the West's arguments for the independence of Kosovo and the invasion of Iraq in 2003 against them. Although everyone in the West considered the votes in the legal action to be illegal and nonbinding, Russia merely pointed to their similar objections to the actions in Kosovo and Iraq. What they did was make their adversaries follow their own rules, and used those rules against them.

Russia outlined a series of steps for their information warfare and fourth-generation warfare. Rather than relying on massive military intervention, the entire Crimea campaign used less than ten thousand actual troops, most of which were naval infantry that had already been stationed in Crimea at the Black Sea base. They did not use tanks and they did not use overwhelming force. After they dealt with the Ukrainian soldiers and their bases, they started their second phase of operations. This was nearly all psychological warfare. Intimidation, bribery, Internet propaganda, media propaganda and an overwhelming information war was waged to prevent any significant resistance force from rising up against them. During this time, they emphasized non-violence from Russian troops, and essentially achieved a clear military victory through a masterfully executed campaign of strategic communication, rather than kinetic warfare.

Russian generals seem to have undergone a thorough revision and substantial change from the way they waged warfare prior to the annexation of Crimea. Influence is now preferable to destruction. Combat without contact is preferable to direct collusion. Disruption of the enemy is far preferable to destruction of the enemy. Cultural warfare is preferable to weaponized warfare. The information component of war has risen above the traditional three-dimensional battlefield.

During the operation in Crimea, the Russian military command shifted the emphasis of its actions to winning the sympathies of society with the help of new organizational developments through information warfare. It used them to suppress the moral and psychological state of enemy military personnel and the civilian populace. Within this framework, the vector of their main efforts has become person-centered, rather than unit- or military-centered. Their main priority was avoiding military force in favor of persuading enemy personnel and pushing them towards activity that supported their own goals and objectives. The cultivation of these societal sentiments combined within a whole range of actions is referred to as "soft power."

The Russian use of soft power included disseminating propaganda, bribing local authorities, and establishing connections with local elites, which allowed them complete control of the operational situation. As a result, the would-be invaders were met with enthusiasm, while the Ukrainian military machine was bogged down with problems of desertion and evasion from their conscripted soldiers.

In the Russian point of view, modern warfare is information warfare. These modern wars take place in the psychological space—as pressure is applied through communications, politics, economics, and technology—suppressing an adversary's will to act. Essentially, they have shifted from a war in the physical environment to war inside the human consciousness. Achieving victory simply means suppressing the enemy's armed forces and suppressing the enemy's civilian population from acting out in the first place. The objective is to minimize the need to deploy hard power while maximizing the use of soft power.

To put it another way, Russians placed the idea of persuasion at the very heart of their operational planning cycle. Russia uses multiple factors to achieve this: psychological operations, external communications, internal communications, massive deception operations, and tactful audience understanding. Clearly they successfully understood the three critical audiences for their actions: ethnic Russians in Crimea, the government of Ukraine, and the international community. They knew their informational target and crafted a specific strategic message which was marketed and tailored to exactly the effect and outcome they required for mission success. Despite the fact that, at the height of the Crimean events, all parties on every side of the conflict actively used similar rhetoric based on the concept of self-determination, self-defense, and sovereignty, only the Russian side turned out to be the one that could effectively support its words with concrete deeds. In this case, mission success was complete battlefield superiority without firing a single shot. Some international analysts referred to it as the "invisible military occupation."

Sun Tzu would be proud.

Chapter 10

Spiking the NFL

When your enemies defy you, you must serve them steel and fire. When they go to their knees, however, you must help them back to their feet. Elsewise, no man will ever bend the knee to you.

—Tyrion Lannister

I always find it strangely funny when liberal celebrities invoke the Constitution and say things like, "We have a right to do this-and-that, and it's guaranteed by the First Amendment!" First of all, they are one hundred percent correct when it comes to their right to protest. They absolutely do have a right to protest in this country, as do all Americans. I firmly support their right to protest, and would fight to protect their rights under the First Amendment.

Yet, is there anything in the Constitution that grants a right to employment? Do citizens of the United States have a right to employment? I've looked through it a few times—from the amendments to the articles—and I just haven't been able to find *a right to employment* anywhere in the Constitution.

This means what President Trump said at the beginning of the controversy that erupted in late 2017 was correct. He specifically said that NFL players should be fired for kneeling for the National Anthem. Do private organizations have the right to fire or employ anybody they want? In the United States, employers can hire and fire employees. Now, firing can be done for any number of reasons. It can be done for obvious intolerance, hatred and bigotry. Of course we stand against hatred, intolerance, and bigotry—but if you want to fire somebody that works for you, there are reasons why you can do so. In this instance, the players were disrespectful to veteran law enforcement and disrespectful to their customers. The customers in the NFL are the people that are watching and attending the games. They're the people who buy merchandise. They're the people who root for their team, no matter what. Those are the customers.

Customers also have rights in the United States. Customers in the United States have the right, for example, to not purchase a product. They can simply say they don't want to purchase this product (or that they don't want to purchase Obamacare—but that's a different subject!). Customers in the United States have the right to vote with their dollars. Just as many vote with their feet, by moving from one state to another. Everyone has the right, quite simply, to not watch ESPN, to not watch the NFL, or to not go to an NFL game. They don't have to go out and buy jerseys, right?

A look at the ratings of ESPN, NBC, ABC and the other broadcasters of NFL games reveals that they're all going down. Way, way down. In fact, it was reported that the entire 2017 season's ratings were down by over ten full percent. I want to expand on that to put it in proper context: The NFL is one of the most popular cultural institutions in the entire United

States. Most political pundits, and others in America, didn't understand why President Trump would make this American institution a target for criticism. Obviously, it didn't relate to a current presidential policy dispute or legislative battle. But what they failed to understand is that the NFL is a powerful cultural institution that touches almost all Americans. There is a massive slice of the American people who love professional football.

When focusing on the NFL, President Trump framed his argument with remarkable simplicity. You're either on the side of the President of the United States, the national anthem The Star-Spangled Banner, and the military, or you are *against* those things. The liberal media elites, the Left, and liberal politicians absolutely lost their minds at this. They knew that Trump was picking a fight he knew he would win, and he was picking it with millions upon millions of Americans. What most people don't remember from 2017 was that President Trump's approval ratings actually increased during the time that he was feuding with the NFL.

This is cultural warfare politics at its finest. President Trump wrapped himself in the flag and framed anyone who disagreed as un-American. For millions of Americans, standing up for the national anthem is something that is hardwired at an early age. Even at little league games, the anthem is played and all in attendance are asked to stand, take off their hats, and reflect for a moment on their country. For civilians, it is probably the most common occurrence throughout day-to-day life that they repeatedly experience the national anthem. For the military, it's played every morning throughout base, and all are required to stop what they are doing and stand at attention. The optics were firmly with Trump on this one. Showing disrespect to the anthem and flag—symbols of America—showed disrespect to America herself. He used that symbolism—used the emotional and cultural weight of the anthem—and he won. Every time another player or owner knelt down, Trump won just a little bit more. In some cases, whole teams refused to even take the field for the anthem. In one instance, Pittsburgh Steeler Alejandro Villanueva took the field by himself for the anthem while his team remained in the locker room. Villanueva served three tours of duty in Afghanistan as an Army Ranger. In 2016 he had said, "I don't know if the most effective way is to sit down during the national anthem with a country that's providing you freedom, providing you sixteen million dollars a year, when there are black minorities that are dying in Iraq and Afghanistan for less than twenty thousand dollars a year." Villanueva's photo went viral.

This episode included some 'inside baseball' with it (pun intended). Donald Trump had something of a pre-existing relationship with Roger Goodell, the NFL Commissioner. Trump once tried to create his own professional football league to compete with the NFL. His was called the USFL. While the league ultimately folded, he is well-known for having made the attempt. I have always thought that it is likely that one of the many reasons Trump picked his feud with the NFL was for it to be a way of taking them down a peg after beating him in that endeavor. Interestingly, during the Trump era, multiple alternatives to the NFL are now being developed. There seems to be a huge market gap for a pro-American football league.

When it comes to the Constitution and the NFL, please understand that the Constitution has no relevance to this situation. Nothing whatsoever that was done or said falls under the purview of the Constitution. If someone thinks that the Constitution says that they can protest whenever they want, it just shows how ill-informed they are. That's not what the conversation is about—and that's not what the President was really talking about. The Constitution doesn't give you a license to do whatever you want. The owners could have said that kneeling during the national anthem is disrespectful to the team and the customer, and anyone who participates in these protests will be cut from the team.

Does an employer have the right to fire someone for making egregious comments while protesting the U.S. national anthem in a stadium? Under the Constitution, an employer has that right.

Now, a lot of other athletes have decided to protest the anthem. If you want to protest the anthem representing the nation that thousands of Americans sacrificed everything for, you absolutely have the right to do so. In the United States, you have the right to be an idiot!

I don't think people like combining politics and sports and that led to a backlash. The NFL is losing money. Ratings are all going down. It's all because this kneeling has made it so incredibly hard to watch sports. Personally, I think if someone really wanted to air their views, they should give a speech—just not on the clock, nor on the playing field. They could also make a documentary or donate money to charity. There are great ways to make your message heard, without bringing politics into the game and without bringing hatred and disrespect to the American flag.

And tweets don't cost anything, right? Nobody has to pay to use Twitter, so if you can tweet about something, why doesn't LeBron James tweet about every time there's a shooting in the inner cities of Chicago, or Baltimore, Los Angeles, Detroit, or Philadelphia? I actually think that LeBron James was just upset because everybody knows that Steph Curry is better than him. He was upset that Steph Curry was getting the spotlight, so he tried to make the story about himself, because he's arrogant. That is what the *real* story is. Steph Curry is one hundred times better as a player than LeBron James.

Several months after this all died down, while appearing at the College Football Playoff National Championship in Atlanta in January 2018, President Trump seized the opportunity for cultural symbolism once again. He appeared on the field with his hand over his heart and sang the national anthem while flanked by ROTC cadets in uniform. Trump won this cultural contest, hands down. Exactly as he'd set it up from the start.

Chapter 11

Polls as 4D Warfare

Dark wings, dark words.

—Varys the Spider

One of the most-used tactics in the mainstream media's toolkit is the use of public opinion polls to shift opinion instead of simply reporting it. The tactic of polls as persuasion can be successful and effective and you'll see it employed again and again and again. At one time, polls were only used to attempt to determine the likely outcome of upcoming elections. Polls were conducted in the immediate run-up to the election, and reporting on them was held as an interesting data point—but not the lofty, pedestal status the polls are given today. Initially, polls were seen as something of a novelty in American politics. There is a common axiom among political consultants that "the only poll that matters is Election Day." As the United States moved into the 21st-century information age, numbers and data suddenly took on a sort of pseudoscientific and mythical status in the Information Environment. This definition of data stems from the technology revolution of the last ten years and the insertion of concepts and ideas—like algorithms, computer programming, and digital environments into our daily lives. Hollywood movies like *Moneyball*, which depict data as having the ability to construct a winning baseball team, show data to audiences as having extremely advantageous benefits, bestowing a nearly magical status upon it.

The media industry spends millions erroneously portraying opinion polls as statistics. But opinion polls are not statistics. Opinion polls are nonscientific, highly subjective, easily manipulated, and broadly misunderstood. At their core, opinion polls are the reactions of a specific group of people to a specific set of questions at a specific time. When analyzing an opinion poll, you must consider all the factors as well as the source of the poll.

Manipulation is easy, as any set of questions can be carefully crafted to obtain certain responses. Any group of people can be plied to produce any set outcome. It's important to understand that the answers given represent not only our reactions to the specific question but reactions to an overall set of questions or line of questioning. Often, questions are asked in high sequence, which also influences outcomes. Current events also affect the outcome and the time a poll is taken will influence the results. Finally, people lie. While not widespread in terms of polling, certain scenarios increase the likelihood of false positives given to pollsters.

The use of polling data is a common technique employed by the media to control the narrative. By presenting what appears to be "scientific," they thinly veil propaganda as trustworthy news. Essentially, many polls that the media runs consist of efforts to pay for their own headlines and they can be crafted to say whatever it is they want.

Some examples of false polling that were constantly repeated in the 2016 election was that Hillary would definitely win or that there was a "98% chance" that she would be elected. This 98% number was also given on Election Day by numerous media outlets. Polls can also be shifted by oversampling of certain groups—typically Democrats—in order to give an example that is more favorable to Democrats. Some polls are used by candidates as fundraising polls in order to generate a favorable outcome for a new fundraising push by that candidate. These polls are most definitely inaccurate, though they are seen as the exception, rather than the rule.

One of the most effective polls and the most accurate polls was the *Los Angeles Times* poll that was conducted throughout 2016, 2012, and 2008. This poll was unique, because it pulled from a source group of three thousand people and, rather than selecting a new group for every subsequent poll, these same three thousand people were polled every day about their preferences in the upcoming election. This poll was derided by many in the mainstream media as being an outlier during 2016, because it consistently showed Donald Trump doing better than Hillary Clinton when compared to any of the other polls out there. There's just one problem with their derision: The *Los Angeles Times* poll was also the most accurate poll in both of Barack Obama's elections. Why was it, then, that this poll was not considered accurate for Donald Trump? That is something the media will have to answer.

The right often fails in the public forum when confronted with polling data or scientific studies. They often believe they are engaged in a Socratic debate where the facts and figures of an issue are to be weighed and discussed in order to find a reasonable solution. This is rarely the case, as the media and the left regularly revert to tactics targeting the emotions of an audience. Rather than complicating the argument with the statistics and figures, it is more effective to simply stay on message and make a point. Do not get into an argument. Stay on message and control the narrative. A famous example of this in action is when Donald Trump was confronted by Don Lemon on CNN about the numbers of rapists entering the United States.

Donald Trump: If you look at the statistics of people com— I didn't say about Mexico, I say the illegal immigrants, you look at the statistics on rape, on crime, on everything—coming in illegally into this country, they're mind-boggling. If you go to *Fusion,* you will see a story about eighty percent of the women coming in, I mean, you have to take a look at these stories and you know who owns *Fusion*? *Univision*! It was in *The Huffington Post*! I said, "Let me get some of these articles, because I've heard some horrible things." All you have to do is go to *Fusion* and pick up the stories on rape, and it's unbelievable when you look at what's going on, so what I'm doing is telling the truth.

Don Lemon: I've read the-, I read *The Washington Post.* I read the *Fusion*, I read *The Huffington Post* and that-, that's about women being raped. It's not about criminals coming across the border or entering the country.

Donald Trump: Somebody's doing the raping, Don. I mean, you know what it's-, I mean, somebody's doing-, they're just saying it's women being raped, well, who's doing the raping? Who's doing the raping? I mean, how can you say such a thing?

CNN's online write-up of the incident won't even publish Don Lemon's response because they know it does not control the narrative. One can imagine a standard think-tank conservative allowing Don Lemon to guide them into the trap of discussing the nuances of the statistics and pontificating on the statistics. The more effective tactic when faced with a situation such as this for any interview subject or debater is to stay on point and stay on message like Donald Trump did in this instance.

Chapter 12

Source Vetting a Curveball

Secrets are worth more than silver or sapphires.

—Varys the Spider

I don't like to talk very much about my experience in the intelligence community for two reasons. First, it is generally something I can't get into, because it's classified and I have a lifelong NDA with the IC. Second, because when I'm making an argument or making a point or informing the audience about news, I don't want to rely on any appeal to authority because of my former rank or position. I would rather have my point rest on the merits of its own credibility as information. However, I can discuss a certain aspect of my former work which is unclassified. I won't share any of the actual content. Instead, I'll share the process for gaining that content. The process that I want to outline is the vetting of sources and how it works.

Source vetting is a continual process. It starts before you even approach somebody. Source vetting is also a holistic process. It's a process that takes place throughout the course of your relationship with a source. Just because a source had good information on Monday doesn't mean they will have good information on Wednesday—but they may. It all comes down to many different factors.

The main thing you need to know before vetting any source or for knowing anything about someone is their placement and access, or "P and A," as it's referred to in the intelligence community. What is this person's placement and what is their access? They're two separate things. "Placement" refers to your job location—your physical placement. "Access" covers the sources of information to which you have access. What programs, what compartments, what doors, or what files can you open?

I'll give you an example: Let's say someone is a janitor at a company or the janitor at the White House. That person's placement is enormous, because he could be walking around and hearing things there all day, or picking up stuff from the trash. (Incidentally, there is a dual shred policy at the White House, so I don't want you to think our hypothetical janitor would have much luck picking through the trash. Information there is strictly destroyed with a cross-cut shredder—meaning it's shredded once horizontally, then shredded again vertically, so you can't piece the bits back together.) A janitor's placement is good, but he doesn't have great access. He may be walking around and hearing stuff, seeing who's meeting who, and see-ing movements. He may be able to say, "This person showed up at the White House today," or "That person showed up at the White House today," but a janitor won't be sitting in meetings or be privy to phone calls.

Another example: What if you just happened to live across the street from the White House? In that case, you could see on a daily basis who went in and out of the visitor's gate. Your access isn't great because you have no idea why they are there, but your placement is good, because you can see them and get an idea of how long they were inside. Now turn it around. If your source is that person going into the White House, then your information is from someone who is actually sitting in the meeting, actually in the room, actually talking on the phone, or reading a transcript of a phone conversation. So, that access is far greater—even if it's only a one-time access.

When it comes down to it, you always have little pieces which reveal what's going on—a piece here from one source, a piece there from another source. To put the picture together, you have to talk to multiple individuals and play them off one another. You have to ask, "What is this source telling me?" and "What is that source telling me?" and "Does it corroborate what the other source said?" If it does, can you go forward with it? Maybe. Maybe it's a medium confidence assessment. Maybe it was a low confidence assessment. Maybe it is a high confidence assessment.

When I talk to a new source and that source gives me information for the first time, as a rule of thumb, I don't run with that initial information. I do this for first-time sources, because I have no idea whether or not what they are telling me is true. I have no idea if they're running a disinformation game on me. I have no idea if it's even verifiable. I've had multiple times where people have reached out to me as sources and then said, "Jack this is going on… this, this and this"—and I'll sit on it.

Now you're going to say, "Don't you want the big scoop? Don't you want the big story? Don't you want to get it out there?" Yes, maybe, but what I'd rather do with a brand-new source is sit on it and wait for validation. You must consider the risk of putting out false information and destroying your credibility. The left will hound you for this and never let you forget your mistakes. Don't give them the ammo. Wait a little while and see what shakes out. If the information they gave me on Monday is proven true on Wednesday, you can start putting them through little tests called source validation.

First you run through basic tests, sticking to the simple stuff. Ask who's going to be in this meeting here, and they might tell you person A, person B, and person C. Then wait for the meeting and see if those three people do, indeed, arrive. If those people arrive, you've just validated your source.

It's a long process and it takes time. You're building relationships. You're validating a source. And when it comes down to it, it's all about *trust*. How do you know you can ever trust another person? Is there any way to really know that you can trust another person? No, it's impossible. It is impossible to fully trust another human being. That's just not the way the human mind works. We do not have telepathic abilities. We are not like "Eleven" from Stranger Things. I can't go into your brain and tell you what you're thinking. I don't ever know, and I'm never going to know, what another person is thinking. However, that doesn't mean that I can't validate and verify the veracity of their information.

That is the process I use to validate the information I get from all of my sources. It's kind of like a scorecard. You must constantly review that scorecard. Sources are humans—they're people with agendas—so you have to validate the strength of what a person is saying, but also consider what their personal vendetta might be. What could that person want in exchange for this information getting out? In politics, it's usually pretty obvious. People will give you information on their political opponents, because they want to defeat them. That happens. If that is the case, then as long as it's true, I don't have a problem reporting it, and I will report it truthfully, and I will probably say that, for example: "This person is anti-Bannon," or "This person is anti-McMaster, anti-Trump, anti-Democrat," and I'll usually put that in my report.

Here's an example a lot of people have asked me about: How did I know that Manafort had been wiretapped months before the media reported it? First, a source told that Manafort was wiretapped and I realized that might be how they knew about the Veselnitskaya meeting. It would make sense that they were listening in. Then I thought, *can I ping this off other sources?* Go back and look at what the first reports of the Veselnitskaya meeting said. It was only reported that Donald Trump Jr. took part in the meetings, but my source told me that it was not just Don Jr. My source told me that it was, in fact, also Paul Manafort and Jared Kushner who took part in these meetings. So, after my source told me that and it was confirmed when Don Jr. came forward with the information, I realized my source actually knew something about the meeting. He had knowledge as to what specifically took place in that meeting that was later reported by other sources and, in this case, confirmed by the subject himself. Now, because my source had been validated, I could move forward with more information on that source, but keep in mind, specifically on that topic only—the meeting. So, I had been able to validate in that case that my source had information on the topic of the meeting between Donald Trump Jr. and Natalia Veselnitskaya.

Never give up your sources.

Once a source is validated one time, that doesn't always mean that the same source is going to be truthful on every single other piece of information that is floating out there in the aether. Every other topic, every other situation, every other potential headline requires a new validation process. You've got to stay one step ahead of everything. You've got to vet every piece of information that comes through. I have still gotten it wrong plenty of times and reported something that came from a source that later turned out to be a bad source. It happens.

As an example, I used to read the website 4Chan. I would search it for information and I got some really good stuff out of it in the past. 4Chan was great when it came to Antifa in their epic unmasking of the Antifa professor with the bike lock at Berkeley. 4Chan was also great when it came to the Macron Leaks. I got the story about French Presidential candidate Emmanuel Macron's emails leaking from a 4Chan post. That was something I originally found on there and then later had vetted by a cyber security expert before publishing it. 4Chan used to be this great place where people would go and drop stories and drop information because it was less well-known and because it was more insular—people knew that was a safe place that you could go and it would be kept anonymous. However, I think what happened is that, as its popularity grew, more disinformation agents from the other side went on to 4Chan and now it's filled with disinformation. Every other post is an anti-Trump post and there are so many lies and so much crap on there that they've poisoned the well.

I've walked away from other disinformation agents when they reach out to me with "paid sources." I turn away from that because we're at a point now where new media is now scoring points on the board ahead of the mainstream media so we have got to up our game.

That's why I don't do satire anymore and it's why I have disavowed trolling. I don't do trolling anymore. It's fun, but there's too much at stake. The president is reading my Twitter timeline. There are many people around the world watching us and looking at our movement to see how we move forward with the America First agenda.

That is why everything that we do—everything that I do—has to be a cut above and better than what the mainstream media does. That's why liberal media attacks me all the time. That's why the liberal media comes down on me and has called me "fake," and called me this, and called me that, because I'm beating them at their own game. They are doing everything they can to gaslight their audience into saying, "Don't listen to Jack Posobiec."

Gaslighting is when you lie to someone by telling them false truths. It's honestly a form of emotional abuse, where you lie to people and tell them things like, "This person... don't listen to them, they're a liar, they're racist, or a Russian disinformation agent... they just make up stuff."

I don't "just make up stuff." I never have. I validate sources. I move forward with information when I can. Many times there is information out there that I wish I could share, but I can't validate it. If I can't validate it, I can't vet it, then I can't put it out. It needs to pass the standards I learned in the military of validating and vetting information.

Investigators are only as good as their relationships, which is only as good as our sources, and sub sources. Those are the relationships you must maintain. You must be a relationship manager, because it's a transactional relationship. You have to find out what your source wants. You have to find out his desires. You have to say, "How can I help you?" I want the information. I'm very upfront about that. I say, "I want the information that you have." You've got to reflect and think about that source as a person, as a human. What does he want out of this? It's not enough to think they just want the truth to get out, though many times that's the case. People have different motivations, so you have to understand them as a person. You have to clearly understand what motivates them to put information out and to want to speak to somebody who is in political media. Ultimately, you have to work with them and you have to put your emotions aside.

Source validation is an ongoing cycle. Politicians ask me about that all the time. "How do you know the source is right? How do you know the source is accurate? How do you know that they are a good source?" Have they given you valid information at one time or not? If they do, do they still have good placement? Do they still have access?

Go look up *Curveball*. The Curveball fiasco led to the Iraq WMD case. The mainstream media fell victim to Curveball. "Curveball" was the codename for the source who was giving the CIA all of the information on Iraq's weapons of mass destruction. It was one source. The guy said he was a former scientist and they could prove that he was a former scientist. He described Iraq's WMD program to the CIA intelligence officers while they wrote it all down. The problem was they failed to validate it. We all remember the UN briefings by Colin Powell. The information provided by Curveball was used to put labels on satellite images of facilities that never were active bioweapons sites, nor mobile bioweapon sites. Because Curveball had limited knowledge of a facility, they assumed he knew everything. What they didn't do was validate his information by finding another source.

When it came down to it, the information was wrong. Curveball, whose true name is Rafid Ahmed Alwan al-Janabi, was looking to apply for asylum in Germany. He was also wanted by Saddam's sadistic son Uday Hussein. Curveball concocted this story and had just enough verifiable facts to get him into CIA reporting. All this has come out since, and it's all been declassified, but I want you to understand that disinformation is out there. In the case of Curveball, that disinformation led to thousands of American deaths and hundreds of thousands of other deaths—and for what?

Understand the importance of vetting your sources.

Chapter 13

Eisenhower Planning

Plans are nothing, planning is everything.

—Dwight D. Eisenhower

One of the most important tools for any culture warrior is the Eisenhower Matrix. While it's been around for many years (obviously), this time management and prioritization system is essential for anyone who wants to be successful in the culture wars, as well as successful in any endeavor. Consider it a key life lesson. If it worked well enough to win World War II, it's good enough for you, right?

So what exactly is the Eisenhower Matrix? Another name for the Eisenhower Matrix is the Urgent-Important Matrix. The system helps you decide on and prioritize tasks by urgency and importance and, in addition, it allows users to sort out less urgent and important tasks which you should either delegate or not do at all.

Dwight D. Eisenhower was the 34th President of the United States from 1953 until 1961. Prior to his election as President, he served as the Allied Forces Supreme Commander during World War II. As if that wasn't enough, he later became NATO's first commander.

With all of that going on, Eisenhower clearly had a jam-packed schedule every day. Any executive does. Time management at that level becomes critical, though everyone will benefit from better time management. His decisions on how to spend his daily 24 hours led to his creation of the Eisenhower Matrix.

Eisenhower stated: "What is important is seldom urgent and what is urgent is seldom important."

Urgent means that a task requires immediate attention right now. These tasks crop up suddenly and scream, "Now, now, now!" at you. Urgent tasks often put you in a totally reactive mode—making you more defensive, rushed, and negative—while causing you to lose focus on the big picture. *Never lose focus on the big picture.*

Important tasks are strategic. They are items that build toward our long-term goals, values, and vision. In a culture warfare context, it refers to your end state. At times, important tasks will also be urgent, but that is more than likely not the case. When you focus on the long-term activities, you operate in a responsive mode, which helps you remain focused, calm, and open to different strategies for dealing with a situation.

It's not an easy distinction to make, and you will often fall into the trap of believing that everything that is urgent is also important, and vice versa.

Smartphones, 24-hour news, and social media constantly bombard us with information and attack our senses. Every stimulus screams, "Urgent!" at us, regardless of its overall importance. What this creates is a situation where you are living in continuous shock. You are always on, and you are always in reactive mode. Is the color of that dress really as important as your long-term goals? Forget it, and focus on the goals.

One change to make—and I can't stress this enough—is to turn off the 24-hour cable news station in the background. It's a constant hum and a constant distraction. They know what they are doing, and they are constantly bombarding you with flashing lights and urgent "BREAKING" news, which typically isn't. Don't let them win. If you want to go a step further, cut the cable cord altogether. You'll save time and money and be able to interact with your family and friends.

Another example that I personally employ: Turn off the ringer on your phone and turn off all notifications for every app. You'll thank yourself.

Use your phone, don't let it use you.

We are living in a golden age for time-shifting. Take ownership of it. Select times you choose to watch a TV series or use social media. Spend time reading, go to the gym, and shut off those incessant interruptions.

Now let's get back to what the Eisenhower Matrix looks like.

The Eisenhower Matrix is a 4-quadrant box that allows you to prioritize tasks and divide them between different strategies:

1. **Do First**

   First, focus on important tasks to be done the same day.

2. **Schedule**

   Important, but not-so-urgent stuff should be scheduled.

3. **Delegate**

What's urgent, but less important, delegate to others.

4. **Don't Do**

What's neither urgent nor important, don't do at all.

I often wonder where Eisenhower would place social media in this classification.

Here's a further breakdown of the quadrants:

Do First is the first quadrant. Do First items are important and need to be done today or within 48 hours, at the latest. Complete these as quickly as possible and do not waste time on them. A lot of people find using a timer helpful while accomplishing these tasks. Social media is great for "going down the rabbit hole," but timers will help with that. There are also specific apps for it.

Be proactive. If you plan and organize, even just a little bit, many Do First tasks become much easier and can sometimes be completely eliminated. For example, instead of waiting until the last minute to work on something you know is due at a certain time, allot your time so it is finished well before the deadline. Another really basic example is regular maintenance of your health, your car, and your house—don't let it become a crisis first (which would make it urgent). As far as your health goes—take care of it. You only get one body.

Decide is the second quadrant. These items are important, but less than urgent. Think of this as items you can put onto your calendar, but don't need to do immediately. Schedule items which do not have a specific deadline, but nonetheless are important enough that you need to complete them in order to move further toward your goals.

These tasks are important, yet not urgent, but there's a secret here: These are actually the most important items on your list from a long-term perspective. Spend as much time as possible in the second quadrant. This is the space for spending time with family, reading, exercising, praying and any other life-enhancing items. Make an investment into them every single day.

Conversely, these items are also what people put off the most. It's all too easy to put them on the back burner and say you'll get to them "someday." The truth is, someday doesn't come by itself. We have to go to it. Stop living in default mode and take ownership of your life. Everyone gets 24 hours in a day—it's up to you how you spend them.

Delegate is the third quadrant. Delegated items are less important to you, but still fairly urgent. You should keep track of delegated tasks by phone or email to check back on their progress later. Picking up the phone is a lost art in our society, but it's the best way to get anything done. Actually connect with a human, instead of sending a cold text message or tweet. It makes all the difference.

One example of an item to delegate could be someone calling you to ask for an urgent favor or request that you attend a meeting. You could delegate this request by recommending a better person for the job or by simply give the person the information or direction to accomplish the item themselves.

Be assertive. A lot of people fall into the trap of spending the majority of their time on items that could be delegated. Remember that these are items that are important mainly to others, not necessarily important to you. They should be done, and working with others and collaborating is essential, but it should not come at the expense of your own goals. This is called the, "Nice Guy Trap." Learn how, and when, to say no.

Delete is the last and final quadrant. I know this is going to hurt, but it's got to be said. Some activities and habits (when done to excess) prevent us from achieving our goals. Don't worry, everyone has this issue, and the demons of the 21st century are constantly seducing us to click on the next shiny object.

You know what these behaviors are. I'm not going to waste your time listing them all out. What I will say, though, is it takes a true adult in command of their lives to know when a time-wasting activity has become too much and when to admit it. Being able to make that admission separates successful people from those who live life set on default. Life has lots of paths that are laid out for us and the majority of people tend to follow them. If you want to be a culture warrior, these paths do not work because you have to color outside the lines.

That said, time-wasting activities can be turned around with multitasking or combining with a Quadrant 2 activity. Watch your favorite TV shows while working out. In fact, make a habit of it, and eventually you will come to associate the interest in that program with working out so much so that it becomes second nature to do so. I'm a big audio book guy, and when I was in the military, people would frequently tease me for this. But if we were going on a 10k run, you better believe I was bringing a good book along for the ride.

Five General Tips of Cultural Warfare Time Management

- Make a To-Do list for the day and stick to it. Not only is it powerfully effective, but it frees your mind up from worrying about what you should be doing. Always prioritize by importance and urgency.

- Do not fill up the quadrants completely. 5 items each is more than enough. Take care of the most important ones. The goal is completing items.

- Make one To-Do list for your professional items and another for personal/family items. Make sure to not ignore one for the needs of the other.

- Do not let anyone else decide for you. Reach out to respected peers and friends for advice. Never let your enemy define your goals.

- Don't spend all your time on time management. The perfect is the enemy of the good.

The Eisenhower Matrix, like everything else in this book, is not a foolproof system for success. No one should attempt to adhere to it rigidly as that is not human. Instead, think of it as an ongoing process, like planning. The more time you set aside for personal and family development, the more you will find yourself succeeding at your other endeavors. The contrary to that is that the less time you spend each day on Urgent items, the less stress you will have, and the more you will be able to accomplish your long-term goals and vision. It goes without saying that time-wasters, while they can be a great way to reduce stress in the short term, are empty calories in the long run. Keep these to a minimum, and you will see immediate results in all your campaigns.

Chapter 14

Flash—It's a Mob!

I fear we might get caught between three armies.

—Kevan Lannister

One of the best and most effective tactics that Trump supporters used in the 2016 election campaign was that of flash mobs. Flash mobs are essentially a cheap, fast, and effective means of showing support for a candidate or position anywhere in the country at any given time. We found that the most successful flash mobs were the ones that were coordinated with other events that were going on, whether that event was a Trump rally or a Hillary rally. Of course, later on in the election, we did not have many opportunities for Hillary rallies, because she stopped doing them due to her many health issues.

A flash mob only needs five or more participants holding signs with similar messaging. That messaging needs to be absolutely clear. Never show up to a flash mob with a sign that has more than five or six words written on it. No one is going to sit there and spend the time they need to read long paragraphs of information that you put together on your poster board. I am sure it is all very interesting and I am sure that you think it really makes a great argument, but I'm telling you right now that it is not going to be read by 99% of the people who see it. Keep it simple. Keep it tight. Keep it professional. In a flash mob, encourage people to look their best, to wear neutral colors, and to let people know that their image is going to be shown all throughout the Internet. This is most effective, because you want to show that your group is good-looking, fun, and positive. Flash mobs are a great way to share positive moral messaging and information warfare.

We also found that, with flash mobs, it didn't always matter exactly what happened on the ground—it only mattered that many instances of flash mobs took place around the country at one coordinated time, or that a flash mob was focused at a specific strategic target. Essentially, flash mobs were a great show-of-force tactic. One of the most effective show-of-force tactics that we found was the narrative of operating behind enemy lines. This was achieved numerous times during the election and immediately after with the following examples: Times Square, the Hamilton musical, the Trump Hotel on Access Hollywood weekend, the Hollywood star, the final Hillary and Obama rally in Philadelphia, and the March on Washington, which was held in October, 2016.

Here's how we made the The March on Washington so successful. We brought about five hundred Trump supporters from around the country together in our nation's capital. Then we marched down the street wearing Trump T-shirts, flying American flags, and loudly and proudly supporting Donald Trump for president. What made this so effective in optics and messaging was that all around us establishment types were looking at us with wide open eyes and mouths agape. They had no idea there were so many Trump supporters in the country and they had no idea while sitting there in Washington D.C. that Trump supporters were that committed to his candidacy. They discovered the whole truth on November 8.

Another example of a successful flash mob, with a twist, was the Shakespeare in the Park episode. In summer 2017, a New York theater group was putting on a presentation of Julius Caesar with the main character changed to portray Donald Trump as president. They also changed his wife to Melania Trump. Halfway through the play, the actor portraying Donald Trump was brutally stabbed on stage with as much blood and gore as any Quentin Tarantino film. Coming on the heels of the Steve Scalise shooting, myself and activist Laura Loomer crashed the production, and Laura herself stormed the stage calling out, "Stop the normalization of political violence!" When Laura was escorted off the stage, I leapt from my seat, calling out "Goebbels would be proud!" in reference to the Nazi propagandist. I was also immediately asked to leave on that crisp summer's night. The incident turned into a firestorm and achieved significant media attention. I still get asked about that one even now. The reason that modified flash mob of Trump support was so successful in messaging and optics was that it used the narrative of operating behind the lines—in this case a liberal theater in the heart of Manhattan—as well as the optic of standing up for peace and peaceful rhetoric in the face of horrific violence. I'll never know if I changed the minds of anyone in that audience or anyone who saw the video, but I will always know that I stood up for peace. Hopefully, that is enough.

Not too long after that I held a rally for peace in Washington D.C. just in front of the White House. The reason I held the

rally for peace, and invited a diverse group of participants—
including Democrats—was to show that Trump supporters, in
general, are not violent. We abhor violence and stand up to
those who would perpetrate it. This issue comes up again and
again for Trump supporters who are routinely attacked by left-
wing violent groups simply for meeting together and having
an assembly with like-minded individuals. Left-wing groups
attack us again and again and the mainstream media barely
even notices. We have always tried to take the high road and
we will always continue to do so. Violence, hatred, and bigotry
has no place within the Trump movement. We have thrown
out bigots and those who call for violence since 2016 and will
continue to do so. We stand for *peace*. It is ironic that the
peace movement began as a movement of the Left. Now the
Left is violent and it is the Right who have usurped the mantle
of the peace movement.

Flash mobs show dispersed support. Flash mobs demonstrate that there is support across the nation and in large numbers. While each specific flash mob itself may not be large
in number, the overall cumulative effect of flash mobs held
throughout the country demonstrates numerical support. This
number of supporters is compounded by the fact that these optics, pictures, and videos are shared throughout social media. It
fosters a sense of community and a sense of motivation among
the movement. It is a morale boost for Trump supporters to
hold a flash mob. Flash mobs are also an example of culture
jamming, because flash mobs in and of themselves are typically
a leftist tactic, akin to protesters holding signs, though in this
case we are holding positive signs.

Flash mobs normalize us in the eyes of the nation. To fully understand what's going on, you have to understand the context in which these flash mobs were taking place. During 2016, the media pushed a narrative to tell voters that Donald Trump was morally and politically unacceptable to vote for or support. Yet a flash mob showed that in practice others were supportive of Trump. This was known as the "silent majority" in the past and, in many cases, is known as the "shy Trump voter" phenomenon. Essentially, what a flash mob shows to people on social media and the people in the community, is that, hey, if these people are brave enough to hold their convictions up high and broadcast their views in public, then perhaps simply voting for Trump within the confines of a private ballot box isn't quite as bad as the media is trying to tell me.

Flash mobs are also prepackaged for media headlines. *Trump supporters hold flash mob outside Trump Tower! Trump supporters hold flash mob outside Hamilton musical on Broadway!* These headlines are not organic. They can be written simply if you think in terms of the headline first and work backwards from there. What headlines do you want to see? Make that your goal and then act out the part.

Flash mobs are an extremely effective optic and extremely effective at showing positive messaging. They are a great way to show your support and will be highlighted across social media and achieve earned media at the same time.

Chapter 15

Gunn Control

Sitting on a throne is a thousand times harder than winning one.

—Robert Baratheon

In July of 2018, Walt Disney Studios—the parent company of Marvel Studios—fired high-profile director James Gunn, the director of the multi-billion-dollar Guardians of the Galaxy franchise, and one of the top directors of the Marvel Cinematic Universe.

Why did they fire him?

He tweeted about child rape.

Repeatedly.

Long before he had ever been involved with superhero films aimed at the family audience, Gunn had posted hundreds of times on social media—on Twitter and elsewhere—about raping children. Gunn claimed those posts were all "jokes." Were they? You be the judge.

Here's the twist:

The tweets were uncovered by Mike Cernovich and me.

Even worse than the tweets were James Gunn's blog posts, which detailed depraved acts performed by animals and children on movie sets. Were these satire? Jokes? Even for those with a crude or taboo sense of humor, these appeared to involve something even darker and different.

Hollywood has literally thousands of reporters, journalists, and commentators focused on star actors and directors. Disney has one of the most thorough vetting processes of any company in the world. Millions of fans pay close attention to every interview, every tweet, every word said by the people who make these popular movies.

So why didn't anyone ever report James Gunn's tweets before?

There were a few factors at play here. They are the New Rules, the #MeToo era, and the Democrat-Media Complex.

I will break down what these mean in terms of the Gunn situation.

First, the Democrat-Media Complex refers to the collusive and symbiotic relationship between the Democrat Party (the Left) and the Media (which here includes Hollywood). In many cases they are all one and the same. Due to the low standards of so-called journalism in 2018, hundreds of thousands of man-hours are spent every week pouring over the social media posts of anyone even remotely associated with the Right.

This has recently begun to include not only right-wing figures and political officials, but also their families. *The Huffington Post* recently led a hate campaign against the family of a conservative Twitter personality, causing her husband to lose his job and her family restaurant to suffer relentless attacks by leftists for no reason other than their familial association.

What the Left has created is a paradigm of binary tribalism whereby anyone not explicitly aligned with them must therefore be on the Right. And as such, any action against them is justified and no quarter is ever given. By the same token, no one on the Left must ever be targeted for reporting or research, and when on occasion the dam does break, every opportunity must be given to protect, defend, and rehabilitate anyone who may have committed transgressions, crimes, or immoral acts, just so long as they are on the Left.

In 2018, Left and Right is chiefly defined by who is or isn't a supporter of President Trump. To many, all nuance has faded away into this simple binary distinction. Keep in mind, these are the same people who claim there are more genders than Baskin Robins has flavors.

In this context, it soon becomes abundantly clear why James Gunn was never targeted for any research or reporting efforts by leftist SJWs. Even the "wokest" blogger at *Buzzfeed* would never do anything to damage the public reputation of someone who hates President Trump as much as they do. After all, that pro- or anti-Trump dividing line is now the only relevant standard for defining anyone—according to the Left. It is this adherence to a binary tribalistic worldview that prevented anyone in media from looking into James Gunn's tweets after the child rape tweets were uncovered, and caused them to immediately began making excuses for him.

Second is the #MeToo Era. This refers to the tectonic shift of Hollywood and the Left now beginning to finally admit that the movie industry was run by some of the most perverted and disgusting people of all time, and to take steps to clean out some of these individuals. A few of the most well-known examples are Harvey Weinstein, Kevin Spacey, and disgraced former Senator Al Franken. In the past, the sex-for-work

Weinstein casting couch was an open secret in Los Angeles and had even been the subject of an open joke at the Oscars. People laughed as Weinstein used his power and influence to essentially push young women into sexual relationships with him. Other women accused him of sexual assault. Now he has lost his company and is under investigation.

Numerous accusers came out against actor Kevin Spacey as well, both male and female. Now he has lost his starring role on his long-running Netflix show and he was replaced by another actor in a movie in which he was starring. Al Franken was forced to resign his Senate seat after photos of him molesting a sleeping female reporter appeared. These incidents, and the public outcry from them which ensued, started a campaign of no tolerance for abusive behavior, whether past or present—a campaign that extends itself to comments as well as actions.

Finally, the era of the New Rules is really what had the most influence on the James Gunn firing over his child rape tweets. Defenders of Gunn use an argument that his tweets were old, and therefore irrelevant, or that he was simply "joking" and that there was no truth to his words. In an earlier time, those explanations may have won the argument.

Not today. Today, thanks to the social media hyperfocus of the social justice warriors and their media enablers, every single person is held to every single word they post, say, or tweet—regardless of when they said it.

President Trump's entire life history is still brought up, repeatedly, as if incidents from 2005 can somehow affect his Presidency in 2018. Most notably, Roseanne Barr was fired by Disney-owned ABC for a single tweet she wrote about a former Obama official, even after apologizing profusely and stating she had not intended her statement the way it was taken.

By contrast, James Gunn deleted 10,000 tweets. Perhaps ironically, the "Roseanne standard" of a single tweet justifying disemployment was strenuously promoted and defended by James Gunn himself. On the same Twitter account with which he'd been cracking jokes about abusing children, Gunn stated that people must be held to account for their bad tweets, and that freedom of speech has consequences—one of which is being fired. Why Gunn did not delete his many, many child rape tweets while calling for Roseanne to be fired is more than a little strange, especially since he was an active cheerleader for her firing.

This, of course, kicked the Left into deploying what I call the First Commandment of the Left: "It's OK When We Do It!"

- Don't bring up James Gunn's old tweets! But we'll define *you* by your old tweets!

- Don't take James Gunn out of context! But Trump admitted he is Hitler and an assaulter!

- Doesn't matter, James Gunn said it ten years ago! Now listen to what Trump said ten years ago!

At the time of this writing, James Gunn has not been rehired by Disney despite a public campaign on his behalf by many major actors and actresses.

However, Disney has launched a major PR push with the entire cast of his Guardians of the Galaxy films releasing an open letter demanding Gunn be rehabilitated because of his "bad jokes" and describing the outrage against him as "conspiracy theories."

But here's what Disney doesn't realize.

They do not understand 4D Warfare.

Disney is Goliath. They are the elephant in the entertainment room. They have billions of dollars and influence over the entire entertainment and news media.

And the entire world has seen Gunn's sick comments already, thanks to the social media propagation effect.

Disney stars and Hollywood celebrities try to act like nothing happened, which only serves to confirm their tacit endorsement of his behavior and comments—in stark contrast to their harsh response to Roseanne, a beloved midwestern grandmother who happens to also support Trump.

Mark my words.

This won't end well.

We're just getting started.

Chapter 16

Rules for 4D Warriors

Print this out. Make a card of it for your wallet. Put it in your purse. Tape it on your desk. Put it on the back of your phone. These are the ways to fight the culture wars and win. Master information warfare. These are the Rules for 4D Warriors.

1. Perception is reality.

2. Optics, Optics, Optics!

3. Stay on the offense.

4. Make the next move. Never rest.

5. Keep your enemy guessing.

6. Brand your enemy before they brand you.

7. Make your enemy live up to their own standards.

8. Lower your enemy's social status.

9. Never use violence except to save your life or the lives of others.

10. Always stand on the side of peace.

11. Never fight where your enemy chooses. Know your terrain!

12. Never let your enemy see you coming, but always let them know you are.

Chapter 17

Go Forth...

As you go forth with this knowledge, stand tall and stand strong. If you use the strategies and tactics employed in this book, you too will become a 4D Warrior.

Here are the last pieces of advice I can offer.

Be hungry. Always be chugging. Every day ask yourself, "What did I do today to move the needle?"

Be inspired. Learn what is going on around you, making note of events and community functions, then go out to them. Film videos. Show the good and the bad. Show the world the mainstream media is ignoring. There are more of us than there are of them.

Be informed. Collect intelligence on your subjects before you appear at an event, write a story, or even send a tweet. Do your homework. Dig deep into your research. This is the golden age of information and it's all out there at your fingertips. Don't think "Google Search" and the first 5 URLs it shows is the end of your research. Don't be CNN. In fact, that is good advice in general: never be CNN.

Be David, not Goliath. Whoever read David and Goliath and identified with Goliath? No one wants to be Goliath. You *want* to be the underdog. You *want* your adversary to be the powerful aggressor. Understand the power dynamics before committing to any action. We are up against billionaires and all we have is our minds, our spirits, and each other.

Be flexible. The perfect is the enemy of the good. Learn the 80-20 rule. Focus on the 20 percent of things that will give you the highest and best return on your time. Accept solutions that are not 100 percent perfect. Not every play has to be a touchdown, and each yard gained is one step closer to victory. It's a marathon, not a sprint.

Be mindful. Do everything in your power to stay on the moral high road. The temptation to step off it is always going to be there—and in the moment may seem easier—but do not do it! The positive strategic effects of restraint will las much longer than any fleeting instant of gratification. When Antifa punches you, defend yourself and stand tall, but do not assault them. Let the police do their job. And get it all on camera. I'm speaking from experience here.

Be imaginative. Use your cunning, your cleverness, your creativity.

Be encouraging. Do not create hierarchies. Instead, seek to empower everyone. Encourage one another, and strengthen one another.

And if you have some ideas about what you think others can do, write a book.

I'd love to read it.

Jack Posobiec, 2018.

About the Author

Jack Posobiec is a former U.S. Navy intelligence officer who deployed with the DIA to Guantanamo Bay and around the world with the Office of Naval Intelligence. He is one of the most effective right-wing activists on social media and is followed by hundreds of thousands of people on Facebook and Twitter. He is the author of *Citizens for Trump: The Inside Story of People's Movement to Take Back America.*

CPSIA information can be obtained
at www.ICGtesting.com
Printed in the USA
LVHW09s1711081018
592815LV00001B/362/P

9 789527 065655